Cricket

by Michèle

Pioneer Valley Educational Press, Inc.

Contents

A Newborn Puppy

Here is Cricket.

Cricket is an Australian Shepherd.

She is only one day old.

She cannot see or hear

because her eyes and ears are closed.

Cricket is one day old. ▶

After Cricket is born, her mother begins to lick her. Cricket is in a small, greenish sack. The licking opens up the sack. Cricket begins to breathe on her own. Soon, Cricket begins to squirm and cry.

Cricket is very tired. Being born
is hard work! For the first few days,
Cricket sleeps a lot.

Cricket's First Family

Here is Cricket's mother.

Cricket's mother knows how to track people.

She can run through obstacle courses,

jump over fences, and run through tunnels.

This is Dancer, Cricket's mother. ▶

Here is Cricket's father.

He is a champion working dog.

He knows how to help the farmer bring the

sheep, cattle, and ducks

to the pasture or the barn.

He lives on a sheep farm in Montana.

This is Cody, Cricket's father. ▶

Cricket has six brothers and sisters.

They like to sleep together in a big pile.

Sleeping together makes them feel

warm and safe.

Eating

Cricket and her brothers and sisters
drink milk from their mother.
This is called nursing.
Cricket pushes a brother aside
to make sure she gets a drink, too.
Cricket is too young to eat dog food.
She does not have any teeth yet.

When Cricket is three weeks old,
she starts to eat puppy food.
She now has small teeth.
Cricket and her brothers and sisters
still drink milk from their mother,
but they love the puppy food, too.

As Cricket gets older,

she begins to explore.

Sniff! Sniff! Cricket smells something.

What can it be?

Is it something to eat?

A Herding Dog

Australian Shepherd dogs help farmers gather their animals together. This is called herding. Will Cricket or any of her brothers or sisters be good at herding? Some ducks are put in a pen with the puppies. Cricket keeps the ducks together and moves them across the pen to a corner. Cricket looks like she will be good at herding animals!

Cricket herds the ducks. ▶

The Kindergarten Visit

When Cricket and her brothers and sisters
are seven weeks old, they visit
a kindergarten class.
The puppies are very excited
to see the children.
The children are very excited
to see the puppies.

Cricket visits a kindergarten classroom. ▶

23

Cricket likes visiting the class.

She runs around the room

and jumps up on all of the children.

She gives the children kisses.

A New Family

Now that Cricket is nine weeks old,
it is time for her to go to live
with her new family.
Cricket's new family will take care of her.
They will feed Cricket and teach her
new things. Cricket will also get
lots of love from her new family.

Glossary

herding: to gather animals together

nursing: to drink milk from a mother

pasture: area of grass for animals

champion: holding first place